The Sassy Bitch's Book of Dirty Jokes

Katie Reynolds

Ulysses Press

Published in the U.S. by
ULYSSES PRESS
P.O. Box 3440
Berkeley, CA 94703
www.ulyssespress.com

First published in the U.K. as **Rude Jokes for Bad Girls** and **Rude Jokes for Bad Girls 2** in 2008 by Carlton Books Ltd.

ISBN: 978-1-56975-698-0
Library of Congress Control Number: 2008911308

Acquisitions Editor: Nick Denton-Brown
Managing Editor: Claire Chun
U.S. Editor: Abby Reser
Front cover design: TG Design
Interior design and production: what!design @ whatweb.com
Illustrator: Anna Hymas

Printed and bound in the United States by Bang Printing

10 9 8 7 6 5 4 3 2 1

Distributed by Publishers Group West

contents

how come?

How do we know God is a man?

If God was a woman, she'd have made sperm chocolate flavored.

Why did Moses wander in the desert for 40 years?

Because even back then men wouldn't ask for directions.

Why did God give women nipples?

To make suckers out of men!

What did Adam say to Eve when he got his first hard-on?

"Take cover! I don't know how big this thing gets!"

What does a Greek bride get on her wedding night that's long and hard?

A new surname.

What did the elephant say to the nude guy?

"It's cute, but can it pick up peanuts?"

What did the typhoon say to the coconut tree?

Hang onto your nuts this is going to be one hell of a blowjob.

What do you do when your husband turns 40?

Try to change him for two 20s.

What happened to the big-titted streaker at the pop concert?

She was thrown out by the bouncers.

Why do married men have strobe lights in their bedrooms?

To create the illusion they've managed to get their wives moving during sex.

Why do guys have a hole in their dick?

So oxygen can get to their brain!

Why do men like microwave dinners?

Because they like their food like their sex – finished in under five minutes.

Why do men like having sex with the lights on?

It makes it easier to put a name to the face.

How can you tell the characters in soap operas are fictional?

In real life, men aren't that affectionate out of bed.

Did you hear about the guy who had a penis transplant?

His hand rejected it.

How can you tell if a lesbian is butch?

She rolls her own tampons.

What's the best thing about being the oldest chick in a biker gang?

You don't have to pull up your T-shirt so far when you're flashing your tits.

How do women get rid of unwanted pubic hair?

They spit it out.

How do you turn your sex toy into a snowplow?

Buy him a shovel.

What's pink, shriveled and wrinkly and hangs out a man's trousers?

His mom.

What do a guy and a secondhand car have in common?

They both have a tendency to misfire.

Why did the man cross the road?

He heard the chicken was a slut.

Why are men like coffee?

The best ones are rich, warm and keep you up all night long.

Why are men like popcorn?
Because they fill a hole, but only for about five minutes.

Why are men like summer vacations?
Because they never seem to last long enough.

What does an elephant use for a tampon?
A sheep!

What's the square-root of 69?
Eight something.

What's the difference between a woman in a church and a woman in the bath?
One had a soul full of hope.

Why are men like cars?
They always pull out without checking to see if anyone else is coming.

What's the difference between tear gas, a raw onion and a two-foot dick?

Nothing, they'll all make your eyes water!

What's the difference between purple and pink?

The grip.

What do men have in common with ceramic tiles?

Fix them properly once and you can walk all over them for life.

Why are women called "birds"?

Because they tend to pick up worms.

Why can't gypsies have babies?

Because their husbands have crystal balls.

Host, to contestant: "In the Garden of Eden, what were the first words Eve said to Adam?"

Contestant: "Gosh, that's a hard one!"

Host: "Well done. Two points."

Five reasons why chocolate is better than sex:

1   You don't get hairs in your mouth.
2   If you bite the nuts, the chocolate doesn't mind!
3   You don't need to fake enjoying it.
4   It won't get you pregnant.
5   It doesn't keep the neighbors awake!

Why do we call it an "orgasm"?

Because it's easier to spell than "Uh-uh-uh-oh-oh-oh-o-o-eeeeeeeee!!!"

What do you call ten naked guys sitting on each other's shoulders?

A scrotum pole!

Why do doctors slap babies' butts when they're born?

To knock the dicks off the clever ones.

Why don't men often show their true feelings?

They don't have any.

Did you hear about the baby that was born half-male and half-female?

It had a penis and a brain.

What's the scientific name for a female-to-male sex change?

A Strapadicktome.

Why doesn't a woman have the brain of a man?

Because she doesn't have a dick to keep it in.

What happened when the chef got his hand caught in the dishwasher?

They both got fired.

Boys, what do you get if you cross your girlfriend with a pit bull?

Your very last blowjob!

How do you get a pound of meat out of a fly?

Unzip it.

What's the difference between a boyfriend and a husband?

About 35 minutes.

What do you call an intelligent, good-looking, sensitive man?

A rumor.

What's a man's idea of safe sex?

A padded headboard.

How can you tell if a man has manners?

He gets out of the shower to take a pee.

Why are men like spray paint?

One squeeze and they're all over you!

Why are men like disposable tissues?

You can pick them up, blow them and then toss them aside.

What's short and gets straight to the point?

A nymphomaniac midget.

What's the difference between "Ooooh" and "Aaahhh!!"?

About three inches.

How do you get a man to stop giving you oral sex?

Marry him.

What's the difference between love, true love, and showing off?

Spitting, swallowing, and gargling.

What do you do if your boyfriend walks out on you?

Shut the door!

Why is casual sex so great?

You don't have to wear heels.

How do you give a dog a bone?

Tickle his balls.

Why does a honeymoon only last seven days?

Because seven days makes a whole week.

What did the Irish spinster always say in her prayer?

"Dear Lord, please have Murphy on me..."

Which two things in the air can get a girl pregnant?

Her feet!

Why can't Stevie Wonder sort his laundry?

He's a man.

What do you call a man with a one-inch dick?

Justin.

Why do men die before women?

Who cares?

My friends said you're not fit to sleep with a pig.
But I stuck up for you. I think you are.

Guy: "I actually have a girlfriend, but tonight I
gave her the evening off."

Girl: "What for – good behavior?"

Guy: "People think I'm a policeman because of
the size of my love truncheon."

Girl: "Oh yeah, I remember Inch High Private Eye!"

Guy: "Y'know, I could fulfill every sexual fantasy you have."

Girl: "Wow! You mean you have a donkey and a Great Dane?"

Guy: "Are you the girl I was kissing at the party last night?"

Girl: "I don't know. What time were you there?"

Guy: "For the sake of the other women in this bar, I think we should leave together – you're making them all look ugly."

Girl: "I think we should stay – you're making all the other men look good."

Guy: "Hey, why don't you and me go out for a drink?"

Girl: "Sorry, I don't date outside my species."

Guy: "Excuse me, but didn't we go on a date once?"

Girl: "It must have been once. I'd never make that mistake twice!"

Guy: "Hey, beautiful. How did you get to be so good looking?"

Girl: "I don't know – perhaps I got your share too!"

Guy: "Why do you bother wear a bra – you've got nothing to put in it."

Girl: "So? You wear underpants, don't you?"

Guy: "I know how to please a woman."

Girl: "Great, I guess that means you're going to leave."

Guy: "I want to give myself to you."

Girl: "Sorry, I don't accept cheap gifts."

Guy: "Can I call you. What's your number?"

Girl: "It's in the phone book."

Guy: "But I don't know your name."

Girl: "That's okay. That's in the phone book too."

Guy: "I've got a 10-inch penis."

Girl: "I find that hard to swallow."

Guy: "Is this seat empty?"

Girl: "Yes, and if you sit in it, so will mine."

Guy: "What radio station would you like me to switch on when I wake up in the morning?"

Girl: "I don't know. What do they play at the hospital?"

I don't know what your problem is, but I bet it's hard to pronounce.

If I throw a stick, will you leave?

I'll bet your birth certificate is a letter of apology from the condom factory.

You're obviously a man of many parts, it's a shame you're so badly assembled.

Why don't you pull your lip over your head and swallow!

Are you wearing a wig? I suppose you need it to cover the lobotomy scars.

Guy: "D'you want to come back to my place and have sex?"

Girl: "Okay. But only if we do 68."

Guy: "What's 68?"

Girl: "You go down on me and I'll owe you one."

Guy: "You look like the kind of girl who's into S & M."

Girl: "I am. In fact I'm already visualizing the duct tape over your mouth."

Guy: "You're one in a million."

Girl: "Yeah, and so are your chances."

Guy: "Has anyone told you you're the most beautiful girl in the room?"

Girl: "Yes, and I didn't sleep with him either."

Guy: "Hi, can I buy you a drink?"

Girl: "Sorry, I'm too busy right now. Can I ignore you some other time?"

Do you still love nature, despite what it did to you?

Some day you will find yourself – and wish you hadn't.

Do you often set aside this special time to humiliate yourself in public?

Oh, do you have to leave so soon? I was just about to piss in your beer.

Take off that stupid mask – Halloween's not for months!

Whatever kind of look you were aiming for, you missed!

Why don't you go and slip into something more comfortable, like a coma?

boys will be boys

A boss brings his secretary home after a dirty weekend. "That was great," he says. "I bet you won't forget that in a hurry." The secretary replies, "I could. What's it worth?"

A man makes an obscene phone call to a girl. "Hello, darling," he gasps. "If you can guess what's in my hand, I'll show you a good time." "No thanks," says the girl. "If you can hold it in one hand, I'm not interested."

An old sailor in a brothel is trying to make love with one of the girls. "How am I doing?" he asks. "Three knots," says the girl. "What d'you mean three knots?" says the old geezer. The girl replies, "I mean you're not hard. You're not in. And you're not getting your money back."

A woman is in bed with her husband's best friend. The phone rings, and the woman answers it. "Okay," she says. "Yeah. That's fine. I'll see you later." She turns to her lover and says, "That was my husband." "Your husband!" shouts the man. "I've got to get out of here!" "Don't worry," says the woman. "He won't be home for hours – he says he's out playing cards with you."

A newly married couple have promised to be open and honest with each other, but the wife still won't tell her husband how many sex partners she's had. "Look," he says. "Just tell me. I've told you how many people I've slept with. It's only fair." "Well, okay then," says his wife. "Now let me think. There was one, two, three, four, five, you, seven, eight, nine ... "

A male doctor and a female doctor meet up at a medical convention. One thing leads to another and they end up in bed. Just before they get started, the woman dashes into the bathroom to wash her hands. After they've had sex, she gets up and washes her hands again. The guy says, "Anyone who washes their hands that much has to be a surgeon." "That's right," say the woman. "I am a surgeon. And I bet you're an anesthesiologist." "Wow," says the guy. "You're right. But how did you guess?" The woman replies, "Because I didn't feel a damn thing."

A soldier is stationed on a remote tropical island. To keep his mind off the beautiful native women, his wife sends him a harmonica and suggests the soldier learns how to play it. The solider writes back and says that he'll practice every night and won't even think of looking at another woman. Six months later the soldier returns home. He dashes upstairs and finds his wife waiting for him, naked in bed. He tears off his clothes and prepares to leap on her. "Darlin'," he says. "I sure have been looking forward to this!" "So have I," says his wife. "But before we get started, will you do me favor?" "Sure," says the soldier. "What d'you want me to do?" His wife throws a harmonica on the bed and says, "Play me a tune."

A traveling salesman books into a hotel and asks the clerk for a single room. As the desk clerk fills out the paperwork, the man sees a gorgeous blonde sitting in the lobby. She looks at him and gives him a flirtatious wink. The man goes over to make her acquaintance, then, after quick chat, he comes back to the reception desk with the girl on his arm. "Fancy that," he says to the clerk. "I just met my wife here. I guess we'll be needing a double room for the night." The next morning, the salesman comes down to settle his bill and finds he owes over $2,000. "How can it be this much?" he yells. "I've only been here for one night!" "Yeah," says the clerk, "But your wife was here for two weeks."

A girl is on a train and a dirty old man sits opposite her. The old geezer gets a bag of prawns out of his pocket and starts eating them, throwing the shells on the floor round the girl's feet. When he's finished, he screws up the bag and throws it at the girl's head. The girl picks up the bag, collects all the pieces of shell and puts them in the bin. Then she pulls the emergency stop. "You silly cow," says the old man. "You'll get a $50 fine." The girl replies, "Perhaps, but when the police smell your fingers you'll get five years."

A couple have four daughters. The three oldest are tall with blonde hair, while the youngest, Debbie, is short and dark. One day the husband is run over by a truck and his wife comforts him as they wait for the ambulance. The husband doesn't think he'll make it – he turns to his wife and says, "Darling, I can't hang on for much longer. Before I die, answer one question – is Debbie my daughter? I always wondered." "Yes," replies his wife. "Of course she's your daughter. I swear it." Hearing this, the husband passes away peacefully. "Phew!" says his wife. "Thank Christ he didn't ask about the other three!"

A man walks into his local bar. One of his friends comes up to him and says, "You put on a great show with your girlfriend last night. You left the light on in your bedroom – we could see everything you two did projected on the curtains! What a show!"

"Afraid not," says the man. "I wasn't even home last night."

A man comes home and finds his wife fucking the mailman. "Gladys!" he shouts. "What are you doing!?" Gladys turns to the mailman and says, "See. I told you he doesn't know the first thing about sex!"

In the beginning, God creates Eve and gives her three breasts. Eve likes living in the Garden of Eden, but she finds her middle boob a real pain. It pushes the other two out and they keep getting in the way of her arms. She complains to God and he fixes the problem. He removes the middle boob and throws it into a bush. Some time later, God comes back to check on Eve again. Eve is fine but she's lonely and wants a mate. "You're right, Eve," says God. "I should have thought of that. I'll create you a mate called 'Man.' Now all I need is something to work with. Let's see ... Where did I put that useless tit?"

A hooker tries to pick up a Salvation Army band member. "Miss," he says. "Are you familiar with the concept of original sin?" "That depends," says the hooker. "But if it's really original, it'll cost you an extra $50."

A flat-chested girl goes out shopping for a bra. She wants a bra in size 28A, but can't find one anywhere. Eventually she comes across a little lingerie shop run by an old deaf woman. "Have you got anything in size 28A?" asks the girl. "What did you say, dear?" says the old woman, cupping her hand to her ear. The girl lifts up her T-shirt and shows the old woman her boobs. "Have you got anything for these?" she says. The old woman peers at the girl's chest and says, "No. Sorry, dear. Have you tried Clearasil?"

A secretary is helping her new boss set up his computer. She asks him what word he'd like to use as a password. Being a bit of a dickhead, he tells her to use the word "penis." She looks at him and says, "Sorry. Not long enough."

Two lap dancers are getting ready for a performance when one notices that the other isn't wearing her engagement ring. "What happened to the ring?" she asks. "Is the wedding off?" "Yeah," says the other. "Yesterday I saw him naked for the first time – he looked really ugly without his wallet."

A husband says to his wife, "I'm getting our phone number changed. Every day this week someone has rung us thinking we're the coast guard." "The coast guard?" says the wife. "Yes," says the husband.

"Some moron keeps calling to ask if the coast is clear!"

A man comes home unexpectedly and finds his oldest friend having sex with his wife. "You asshole!" he shouts. "I've known you since I was ten years old. We went to school together. We were in the army. I saved your life. You were the best man at my wedding ... Hey! Stop doing that while I'm talking to you!"

A man goes to a massage parlor and pays for a half-hour session. As the masseuse rubs the man's chest she notices he's developed a huge erection. She leans over and whispers, "Would you like to take care of that?" "Yes, please," replies the man. The girl slips out of the room and the man waits in anticipation. A minute later she sticks her head round the door and says, "Have you finished?"

An Italian girl is going on her first date. Her mother warns her about boys. "They're only after one thing," she says. "Don't let him take any liberties. Don't let him feel your chest or your legs. Don't play with his privates, and don't ever let him get on top of you – if you do that you will disgrace your family." When the girl returns, her mother asks her how it went. "We got soaked in the rain," says the girl. "So we had to go to his house and take our clothes off to dry them." "Mamma mia!" says mother. "It's okay," says the girl. "I didn't let him feel my chest or my legs. And I didn't play with his thingy. But when I said I wouldn't, he started playing with it himself and then he said we ought to lie down." "Mamma mia!" says mother. "Don't tell me you let him get on top of you and disgrace your family. "Oh no," says the girl. "I remembered what you said, so I got on top of him and disgraced HIS family."

A husband and wife are arguing. The husband shouts, "When you die, I'm getting a headstone that says, 'Here lies my wife – cold as ever.'" "Oh yeah?" she replies. "Well, when you die, yours will read, 'Here lies my husband – stiff at last!'"

A man comes home and finds his wife in bed with another man. He takes out a gun and shoots him. His wife says, "Look. If you keep doing that you're not going to have any friends left at all!"

A man walks into a pharmacy owned by a couple of old ladies. "I have a problem with my penis," he tells them. "It's ten inches long and always stays hard, even after having sex for hours at a time. What can you give me for it?" The spinsters whisper to each other. Eventually they come to a decision.

One says, "The best we can offer you is $800 a week and a 30% share of our store."

Little Suzie tells her friend that her dad has two dicks. "That's impossible," says the friend. "No it's not," says Suzie. "I've seen them." "So what do they look like?" asks the friend. Suzie says, "One's small, white and floppy, and he uses it for peeing. And the other's long, stiff and pink, and he uses it for brushing mommy's teeth."

Size Chart

9 inches   Oh shit, ouch!

7 inches   Oh yes, mmm!

6 inches   That'll do nicely, thank you!

5 inches   Mmm, yeah ok!

4 inches   Could you try pushing a little more?

3 inches   Is it in yet?

2 inches   Oh forget it! Just use your tongue!

A man goes to see his doctor. "My dick has holes all up and down the sides," he says. "When I go to the toilet it sprays out everywhere. Can you help me?" The doctor looks at the man's perforated dick and hands him a business card. "Is this a specialist?" asks the man. "No," says the doctor. "We can't cure it. But the guy on the card is a clarinet tutor – he can teach you how to hold it."

What is the difference between men and pigs?

Pigs don't turn into men when they drink.

What do a clitoris, a birthday, and a toilet bowl all have in common?

Men usually miss them.

What's the average guy's idea of foreplay?

30 minutes of begging.

What do you call a guy whose missing 95% of his brain?

Castrated.

As the result of a surgical mix-up, a female brain cell happens to end up in a man's head. The brain cell looks around inside the skull – the place seems deserted. "Hello!" she shouts. "Is there anyone here?" There's no answer, so the brain cell shout out louder. "Hello! Is anyone there?" Suddenly she hears a faint voice calling up from the man's crotch. "Hi! We're all down here...!"

Ten Things You Probably Shouldn't Say To A Naked Man

1   Oh! Never mind! I think they have surgery to fix that.

2   My brother has one just the same. He's five years old.

3   Well, this explains your car...

4   Stay there! I'll get my tweezers.

5   Hey! Isn't there a tower in Italy like that?

6   Was your dad a pygmy?

7   Did you ever date Lorena Bobbitt?

8   Is it that cold in here?

9   Is that some sort of optical illusion?

10 Okay. So where did you put the rest of it?

Men and women have different views about sex and relationships: women want a relationship without the complication of unnecessary sex; men want sex without the complication of an unnecessary relationship.

A man goes to a doctor with an orange dick. "That's extraordinary," says the doctor. "Do you work with dyes or other chemicals?" "No," says the man. "Do you work near radioactivity?" asks the doctor. "No," says the man. "I don't work at all. I'm unemployed." "So what do you do all day?" asks the doctor. The man replies, "Mostly I sit on the sofa watching porn and eating Cheetos."

What's the quickest way to a man's heart? Through his rib cage.

Definition of a man: a life-support machine for a dick.

What's the main difference between men and women?

A woman wants one man to satisfy her every need; a man wants every woman to satisfy his one need.

What makes men chase women they have no intention of marrying?

The same urge that makes dog chase vehicles they have no intention of driving.

The government has just announced it will be introducing a penis tax – the only tax men will willingly overpay.

A religious man wants to find a "pure" woman to marry, so he invents a test to see how much his dates know about sex – when he's next out with a girl he'll show her his dick and see how she responds. On his next date, the man suddenly whips out his dick out and says, "What's that?" The shocked woman says, "That's a cock." "You slut!" says the man. "If you were pure you wouldn't know what to call it." The next week he goes on a date with another woman and, again, whips out his dick. "What's that?" he says. The blushing woman responds, "Well, I'd call it a penis." "Hah!" says the man. "If you were pure you wouldn't know what it was, you whore." The man goes on yet another date, but this time when he whips out his dick the woman just giggles. "What's that?" says the man. The girl titters and says, "Well I guess that's what my mommy would call a 'pee-pee.' I don't know though, I haven't seen one before." This is good enough for the man, so he asks her to marry him. On their wedding night, his bride asks to see his pee-pee again. "Look," says the man. "Since we're married now, you can stop calling it a pee-pee. Call it a 'dick.'" "Oh, you big silly," giggles the bride.

"That's not a dick. A dick is ten inches long, three inches wide and black."

A man is in a casino playing the slot machines when his wife rings him on his cell phone and tells him to come home. "I can't leave now," says the man. "I'm on a winning streak. I've got a pile of quarters as tall as my dick." "What!?" shouts his wife. "You mean you're down to three dollars?"

Men are like miniskirts: watch out or they'll creep up your legs.

Men are like public toilets: the good ones are engaged and the rest are full of crap.

Men are like trains: they always stop before you get off.

Men are like bananas: the older they are, the softer they get.

A man marries a girl from a very sheltered background. On their first night together he shows her his dick and, thinking it might stop her playing around in the future, tells her it's the only one in the world. A week later his bride says, "You remember that thing you showed me? You said you had the only one in the world." "That's right," replies the man. "Well, it's not true," says the bride. "The man next door has one as well." The man thinks quickly and replies, "Well, yes, I used to have two, but that man is such a good friend, I gave him one of mine." His wife whines, "Awww, but why did you have to give him the best one?"

A married couple are broke and the only way they can make some money is if the wife becomes a prostitute. The wife puts an ad in the paper and gets her first client. She takes the man into her bedroom and he asks how much she charges for sex. The wife doesn't know, so she goes downstairs and asks her husband. "Tell him it's $100," he says. Back upstairs the wife tells the man the price, but he tells her he only has $40. The wife goes downstairs and asks her husband what $40 can buy. "Tell him $40 is the price of a blowjob," says the husband. The wife goes upstairs, tells her customer what he'll get for $40, and the man starts to strip. The man drops his pants and the wife's eyes pop out at the huge size of his dick. She runs downstairs and says to her husband, "Hey, can you lend me $60?"

Mrs. Cohen, Mrs. Levy, and Mrs. Levine are talking about their sons. Mrs. Cohen says, "My Benjamin is a very successful lawyer. He has a penthouse apartment in L.A., and a summer home in the south of France." Mrs. Levy says, "Well let me tell you about my Samuel. He's a famous doctor who was nominated for a Nobel Prize." Mrs. Levine says, "Well, my Isaac might not be rich or famous, but his dick is so long, ten pigeons can perch on it in a line." Mrs. Cohen says, "Actually, I should confess. I was exaggerating. My Benjamin's an up-and-coming lawyer, but he doesn't have a penthouse or a summer home." Mrs. Levy says, "I've got a confession too. Samuel is a wonderful doctor but he's never won a Nobel Prize." Mrs. Cohen and Mrs. Levy look at Mrs. Levine. "Well, okay," says Mrs. Levine. "So the last pigeon has to stand on one leg!"

A guy snuggles up to his girlfriend and says, "Hey, why don't we try a different position tonight?" "What a great idea," says the girlfriend. "I know – you stand by the sink while I sit on the couch and fart."

Men are like chocolate: they're sweet, smooth, and usually head right for your hips.

Men are like copy machines: you only need them for reproduction.

Men are like secondhand cars: they're cheap, easy to find and unreliable.

A woman hears a knock on her front door. She opens it and finds a young homeless guy begging for spare change. She's about to shut the door when she notices the guy's huge shoes. She remembers the story that men with big feet have equally big penises, so she invites the man in. Next morning the homeless guy wakes after a night of sex and finds $50 and a note pinned to his pillow. The note reads, "Buy some shoes that fit!"

The king of Spain, the king of France, and the king of England are standing on a stage. They're having a competition to see who has the biggest dick. The king of Spain drops his pants. The people see his big dick and shout, "Viva España!" The king of France drops his pants. The people see his huge dick and shout, "Vive la France!" Last, the king of England drops his pants. There's a stunned silence, then the people cry, "God save the queen!"

Two old ladies go to the zoo where they see an angry male elephant running about with a huge erection. "Oh dear," says one old lady. "D'you think he'll charge?" The other old lady looks at the elephant's crotch and says, "Well, yes. I think he'd be entitled to."

Two guys are on a beach. One of them is getting a lot of attention from the girls, and the other guy can't understand why. The first guy reveals his secret. "It's easy," he says. "Just drop a potato down your swimming trunks and walk around for a bit. The girls will be lining up." The second guy takes this advice, stuffs a potato down his trunks, and parades up and down the beach. Things do not go well however, and the ladies are not impressed at all, in fact, they seem to want to keep as far away from him as possible. Baffled, the guy goes back to his friend who immediately sees the problem, "You're meant to put the potato down the front of your trunks ... "

What's pink and drags along the bottom of the sea?

Moby's dick.

What's white and 12 inches long?

Absolutely nothing!

A woman in a card shop spends 20 minutes browsing the shelves, but she can't find what she wants. Eventually she goes to the manager and says, "Excuse me. Do you have any 'Sorry I laughed at your penis' cards?"

A man is embarrassed about the size of his dick and worried that his latest girlfriend will think it's too small. Eventually he decides to reveal the problem. While they're kissing on the sofa, he unzips his pants and guides her hand inside. "No thanks," says the girl. "I don't smoke."

Eight More Things You Probably Shouldn't Say To A Naked Man

1 Ah, isn't it cute!

2 Why don't we just cuddle?

3 It's more fun to look at.

4 Tell you what, why don't we skip straight to the cigarettes?

5 At least this won't take long.

6 I hear too much jerking-off makes it shrink.

7 But it still works, right?

8 I didn't know they came that small.

A mother and daughter are talking about the facts of life. The girl says, "Mommy, what's a penis?" Mother replies, "That's what your father pees with." The girl says, "So what's a prick?" Her mother says, "That's the part that's attached to the penis."

blondes have more fun

A handsome Italian picks up a blonde in a Naples nightclub. He talks her into bed and they spend 20 minutes having energetic sex. When he's done, the Italian lights a cigarette. "You finish?" he asks in broken English. "No," replies the blonde. The Italian wants his new lady friend to be satisfied so he starts again. After 40 minutes, the girl seems to have had enough. "You finish?" says the Italian. "No," replies the blonde. The astonished Italian has another go. He gives it all he's got and uses every trick in the book. After 50 minutes, he collapses beside the blonde. "Are you finish?" he gasps. "No," replies the blonde. The Italian can't believe it, but his reputation is at stake, so he launches into one final effort. Finally, after an hour of high-octane sex, the shattered Italian croaks, "You, you finish now?" "No," replies the blonde. "What?" says the Italian. "How can you not be finish?" The blonde replies, "Because I'm Swedish."

A blonde goes to see her doctor after an operation. "Doc," she says. "How long do I have to wait before I can start having sex?" "You could have it now if you wanted," replies the doctor. "Y'know, that's the first time anyone's asked me that after having their tonsils out."

Have you heard about "blonde paint"?
It's not very bright, but it's cheap and spreads easy.

How does a blonde hold her liquor?

By the ears.

A blonde, a brunette and a redhead are locked in a jail cell. The redhead takes out a harmonica and says, "At least I can play some music and pass the time." The brunette pulls out a deck of cards and says, "We can play games too." The blonde pulls out a packet of tampons and says, "And these are going to be great fun!" "What do you mean?" asks the redhead. "Those don't look fun to me." "Of course they are," says the blonde. "On the packet it says we can use them to swim, play tennis and ski."

What did the blonde's mother say to her before she went out on a date?

"If you're not in bed by midnight, come home."

What do blondes put behind their ears to attract men?

Their knees.

I'm blonde, what's your excuse?

Two blondes are visiting a zoo when they come across a gorilla sticking its huge erection through the bars of its cage. One of the blondes reaches out to have a feel, but the gorilla grabs her and drags her into its enclosure. The gorilla then has sex with the blonde for an hour while the zoo staff run around trying to find a vet to tranquilize him. Eventually, someone shoots a dart into the sex-crazed gorilla and it collapses. The blonde is rescued and rushed to hospital. A couple of days later the blonde's friend drops by to see how she is. "Are you hurt?" asks the friend. "Am I hurt?"

sobs the blonde. "It's been two days and he hasn't called, he hasn't written ... "

What's the difference between a blonde and a jumbo jet?

Not everyone's been in a jumbo jet.

What does a blonde do first thing in the morning?

She introduces herself and walks home.

What's the mating call of the blonde?
"I'm so drunk."

What's the mating call of the ugly blonde?
"I said, 'I'm sooo drunk!!!'"

Brunette: "My boyfriend bought me flowers for Valentine's Day. I guess that means he'll want my legs in the air."

Blonde: "Why? Don't you have a vase?"

Why is a blonde like a good bar?
Liquor in the front, poker in the rear.

A blonde goes to see her doctor. She has really bad constipation and her doctor gives her a course of suppositories to cure it. After two weeks, the blonde still hasn't had a crap so she goes back to the doctor. "I'm surprised," says the doc. "Those suppositories usually work like a charm. Have you been taking them regularly?" "Of course, I have," snaps the blonde. "What d'you think I've been doing – sticking them up my ass?"

What do you get when cross a lawyer with a blonde?

I don't know, but it sure enjoys screwing people.

A dumb-looking blonde walks into a doctor's office. The doctor is a horny pervert. He tells her to strip and then starts stroking her legs. "Do you know what I'm doing?" asks the doctor. "Um? Checking for varicose veins?" replies the blonde. Then the doctor starts rubbing her boobs. "D'you know what I'm doing now?" he says. "Duh? Looking for lumps?" replies the blonde. Then the doctor tells her to lie on the examining table and climbs on top of her. "Do you know what I'm doing now?" asks the doctor. "Yeah," snaps the blonde. "Getting crabs – that's what I'm here for!"

great big long ones

A man sunbathes in the nude and ends up scorching his dick. He goes to his doctor who advises him to bathe it in cold milk. That evening his wife comes home and finds him standing by the kitchen table with his lobster-red dick stuck in a glass of milk. "Oh, right," she says. "I always wondered how you reloaded those things."

A Texan goes into a tailor's to get measured for a suit. "What's your waist size?" asks the tailor. "40 inches," replies the Texan. "We grow them big in Texas." "What's your outside leg?" asks the tailor. "54 inches," replies the Texan. "We grow them big in Texas." "How much space do you need in the crotch?" asks the tailor. "I'm a three-incher," replies the Texan. "Three inches?" laughs the tailor. "I'm four inches and I'm from California." "Hold on, sonny," replies the Texan. "We measure it different where I come from – that's three inches from the ground."

The ten things men know about women:

1. ----------
2. ----------
3. ----------
4. ----------
5. ----------
6. ----------
7. ----------
8. ----------
9. ----------
10. THEY HAVE BOOBS!

A platoon of Marines is having a medical inspection. Their sergeant tells them to strip and line up three rows outside the medical hut. The sergeant sees a man in the back row scratching his arm. He hits the man's elbow with a stick. "Did that hurt?!" shouts the sergeant. "No, sir!" replies the soldier. "Why not?!" shouts the sergeant. "Because I'm a Marine, sir!" yells back the soldier. The sergeant then sees a man in the middle row rubbing his nose. The sergeant hits the man on the head. "Did that hurt?!" yells the sergeant. "No, sir!" is the reply. "Why not?!" shouts the sergeant. "Because I'm a Marine, sir!" yells back the soldier. The sergeant then sees a man in the front row with a huge erect dick sticking out between his legs. The sergeant whacks the end of the erection with his stick and yells, "Did that hurt soldier?!" "No, sir!" replies the soldier. "Why not?!" shouts the sergeant. The soldier says, "Because it belongs to the man behind me, sir!"

A woman takes her two dachshunds, a male and a female, to the vet for a check-up. "Has the male been neutered?" asks the vet. "There's no need," replies the woman. "At home I keep the female upstairs and the male downstairs." "Can't the male climb the stairs?" asks the vet. "No," replies the woman. "Not when he's got a hard-on."

On his retirement, a Jewish doctor who specializes in circumcision takes all the foreskins he's saved over the years and sends them to a luggage maker. He wants all the foreskins turned into a bag as a retirement present to himself. A week later the doctor returns and the luggage maker gives him a wallet. "I gave you all those foreskins and you made me a wallet?" exclaims the surgeon. "I wanted a bag at the least." "It is a bag," says the luggage maker. "If you stroke it, it turns into a briefcase."

After spending years in the closet, Luigi decides it's time to come out to his Italian mamma. He finds her in the kitchen and tells her he's gay. Mamma is shocked. "Luigi!" she says. "You mean you don't like girls?" "No mamma," says Luigi. "You mean you do all those dirty sex things with other men?" says mamma. "Yes, mamma," says Luigi. "You mean you even put other men's dicks in your mouth?" asks mamma. "I do, mamma," says Luigi. "I understand," says mamma. She sighs deeply, then picks up a wooden spoon and starts whacking Luigi over the head with it, "So you put men's dicks in your mouth, and you still have the nerve to complain about the taste of my lasagne..."

What's a man's idea of foreplay?
Brushing his teeth.

Two guys are changing in a locker room. The first guy shows off his huge dick. "It's a beauty isn't it," he says. "It's a transplant job. It cost me $15,000." A few months later, the same two guys meet up again in the locker room. The second guy drops his pants and shows off his new dick. "They cheated you when they sold you your transplant," says the second guy. "I had this one fitted last month and it only cost me $1,000." The first guy peers at the other's dick and says, "No wonder it was so cheap – that's my old one!"

Johnny's mom asks his dad to tell him about the birds and the bees. Dad sits Johnny down in front of the television and puts on a hardcore porn DVD. After a few minutes, Dad points to the screen and says, "You see all that? Birds and bees do that as well."

John has his wife's name, Wendy, tattooed on his dick, but normally, he can see only the first and last letters, "W" and "Y" – he sees the whole name only when he has an erection. One year, John and Wendy go on holiday to Jamaica. They go on a minibus tour of the coast and stop off at lunch time for a rest-stop. John goes to take a piss and finds himself standing next to the minibus driver. John looks down and sees that the driver also has the letters "W" and "Y" tattooed on his dick. "Excuse me," says John, "but I couldn't help noticing your tattoo – does it say 'Wendy' like mine?" "No," says the driver. "I work for the tourist board. My tattoo says, 'Welcome to Jamaica, my friend, have a nice day.'"

A cucumber, a pickle and a penis are moaning to each other. The pickle says, "My life is terrible. When I get big, fat and juicy they're going to stick me in a jar full of vinegar." The cucumber says, "Yeah? Well when I get big, fat and juicy, they're going to slice me up and toss me in a salad." The penis says, "You think that's tough? Whenever I get big, fat and juicy, they put a bag over my head, shove me in a wet, dark, smelly room and make me to do push-ups until I puke!"

Which is easier to make, a snowman or a snow-woman?

A snow-woman! With a snowman you have to hollow out his head and make the extra snow into a pair of testicles.

What do you call a man who's just had sex?

Anything you like – he's fast asleep.

A fireman tells his wife about the new system they have at work. "Bell one rings and we all put on our jackets," he says. "Bell two rings and we slide down the pole, and when bell three rings we're on the fire truck ready to go." "So why are you telling me all this?" asks his wife. Her husband replies, "Well, from now on, when I come home and say 'Bell one,' I want you to take your clothes off. When I say 'Bell two,' I want you to jump into bed. And when I say 'Bell three,' we're going to screw all night." So the next night the fireman comes home and yells, "Bell one!" His wife promptly strips off. Then he shouts, "Bell two!" And his wife jumps into bed. Then he yells, "Bell three!" and they begin having sex. Suddenly his wife yells, "Bell four!" "What the hell is Bell four?" asks her husband. "Roll out more hose!" she shouts. "You're nowhere near the fire!"

An American, an Australian and a German are bragging about how long their dicks are. To see who has the biggest, they go to the top of a 15-story building and flop their tackle over the side. The German goes first and his dick dangles down to the tenth floor. The Australian goes next, and his flops down to the fifth floor. The American goes last, but as soon as his dick has gone over the side he starts dancing around and jerking his hips about. "What are you doing?" asks the German. The American replies, "I'm dodging traffic!"

A man goes to a doctor and asks him to take a look at his dick. "But promise you won't laugh," says the man. "I'm very sensitive about my penis." The doctor agrees, but when the man drops his pants the doctor can't help laughing – the dick is miniscule. "I'm sorry," he says. "But that's the smallest penis I've ever seen. It's so tiny, I can barely see it. So what seems to be the matter with it?" The man replies, "It's swollen."

What do you do with a guy who thinks he's God's gift to women?
Exchange him.

What's the toughest part of a man's body?
His dick. Because it can stand up to any cunt!

What do all men at singles bars have in common?

They're married.

What's the worst part of a man's body?

His dick – it has a head with no brains, hangs out with two nuts, and has an asshole as a next-door neighbor.

Teacher asks her class for a sentence with the word "contagious" in it. Little Suzie sticks her hand up. "My dad and I were driving along, when we saw a fruit truck that had spilt melons all over the road. The driver was trying to put them back in the truck, and dad said it would take that contagious to pick them all up."

An old lady goes to see a doctor about a problem with her sex drive. "I don't seem to have as much fun in bed as I used to," she says. "I see," says the doctor. "And how old are you and your husband." "I'm 82," says the old lady. "And my husband is 77." "And when did you first notice the problem?" asks the doctor. The old lady replies, "Twice last night and once again this morning."

A man walks into a store and asks for a tub of vanilla ice cream, a tub of strawberry ice cream, and a tub of chocolate ice cream. "Sorry," says the woman at the counter. "We're out of chocolate ice cream." "Okay," says the man, "I'll have a tub of tutti-frutti, a tub of coffee and a tub of chocolate." "Are you deaf?" says the woman. "I just told you, we don't have any chocolate ice cream." "Okay," says the man. "Then I'll have a tub of toffee, a tub of rum-raisin, and a tub of chocolate." "Listen," says the woman. "What does the V-A-N in vanilla spell?" "Van," says the man. "That's right," says the woman. "And what does the S-T-R-A-W in strawberry spell?" "Straw," says the man. "Fine," says the woman. "So what does the F-U-C-K in chocolate spell?" The man says, "There's no fuck in chocolate?" "That's right!" says the woman. "And that's what I've been trying to tell you!"

An old geezer stumbles through the door of a brothel. The doorman stops him. "What are you looking for, grandpa?" he says. "You sure you're in the right place?" "Is this where all the hot women are?" says the old man. "Because I'm after a good time." "How old are you, pop?" asks the door-man. "I'm 92," replies the old man. "92!" says the doorman "Boy, you've had it, gramps." The old man looks confused. "I have?" he says, taking out his wallet. "How much do I owe you?"

A farmer and his son go to the market to buy a cow. The farmer finds a cow he likes and examines it all over: he strokes its belly, rubs its back and legs, and even peers up its rear end. "You see, son," explains the farmer. "If you're going to pay for something, you have to give it a real good going over to see if it's worth the money." Next day, the boy runs up to his father and says, "Dad! Dad! I just saw mommy and Uncle Jack behind the barn. I think he's planning on buying her!"

A girl throws a costume party where everyone has to come as a human emotion. The first guest arrives covered in green paint with the letters N and V painted on his chest. "So what are you?" asks the hostess. "I'm green with envy," says the guest. Next to arrive is a woman in a pink body stocking with a feather boa wrapped around her boobs and pussy. "And what emotion are you?" asks the hostess. The woman says, "I'm tickled pink." Next up are two of the hostess's Jamaican friends, Wardell and Delroy. Wardell is naked and has his dick stuck in a bowl of custard. Delroy is also naked, but his dick is stuck in a pear. "I give up," says the hostess. "What emotions are you?" "It's easy," replies Wardell. "I'm fucking disgusted, and Delroy has come in despair."

Teacher reminds her class about an important exam that's taking place the next day. "I won't accept any excuses for absences tomorrow," she says. Billy, the class clown sticks up his hand. "Miss," he says. "What would you say if I called in tomorrow and said I was suffering from sexual exhaustion?" Teacher replies, "In that case, Billy. I'd tell you to come into school and do the test with your other hand."

A couple and their son live in an apartment in the city. One Sunday the couple decide to have an afternoon quickie and ask the son to stand out on the balcony and tell them what's going on in the neighborhood. They figure this will give them some privacy and keep him occupied for a few minutes. The couple go to their bedroom and the son begins his commentary. "There's a car being ticketed by the school," he says. "An ambulance and a police car just drove by. They're having a sale at the sofa store. An old lady is feeding the birds." A few moments later he calls out. "I just saw the priest. And Mr. and Mrs. Carter are having sex."

Mom and Dad rush out of the bedroom. "What?" cries mom. "How do you know the Carters are having sex?" The son replies, "Because their son is standing out on the balcony too."

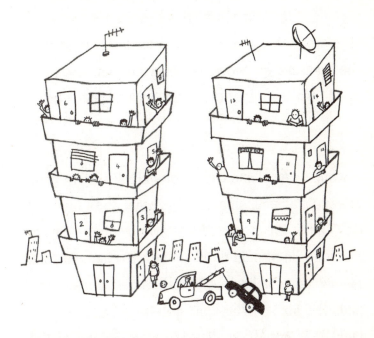

78-year-old Hilda announces that she's going to marry her 19-year-old window cleaner. Hilda's doctor hears about this and goes to visit her. "I think you ought to reconsider this marriage," he says. "It could be very dangerous. Prolonged sex with a young man could be fatal." Hilda shrugs and says, "If he dies, he dies."

A man finds a magic lamp. He rubs it and releases a genie. "What is your wish?" asks the genie. "I love sex," says the man. "So I want to be hard all the time, and get more ass than any man who ever lived." So the genie turns him into a toilet bowl.

A woman complains to her boss that a co-worker is sexually harassing her. "So what does this guy do?" asks the boss. The woman replies, "Every morning he stands right up next to me and tells me my hair smells nice!" "Well, that sounds okay," says the boss. "Why don't you take it as a compliment?" "I would," replies the woman, "except the little creep is a midget!"

Teacher says to her class, "Who can tell me the meaning of indifferent?" Little Suzie puts up her hand. "It means 'lovely,' miss." "No. That's not right," says teacher. Suzie replies, "Yes it is, miss. Last night I heard mommy say, 'That's lovely,' and daddy said, 'Yeah, it's in different.'"

A horny mouse comes across a female elephant with a thorn in her foot. "I can pull that thorn out," says the mouse. "But I'll want a favor in return – I want to have sex with you." The elephant tries not to laugh. "Well, okay," she says. "If you can get the thorn out, you can do what you like." So the mouse pulls out the thorn, and then climbs up on a tree stump to collect his reward. The elephant backs into position. "Let me know when you've finished," says the elephant. The mouse prepares to get started. At that moment, an eagle flying overhead loses its grip on a turtle it's been carrying. The turtle plummets down and hits the elephant on the head. "Ouch!" says the elephant. "Oh yeah," says the mouse. "Yeah. You like that, don't you, baby ... "

Two women are playing golf. One of them tees off, but the ball slices sideways and hits a man standing nearby. The man clasps his hands together over his crotch and falls to the ground in agony. The woman rushes over. "I'm sorry," she says. "Please let me help. I'm a physical therapist. I know just what to do." So the woman pulls down the man's pants and starts giving the man's privates an expert massage. After a few moments the man seems to have calmed down. "How does that feel?" asks the woman. "That feels great," says the man. "But I think you broke my thumb."

To save money, Susan and Tony have their honeymoon at a bed and breakfast run by Susan's mother. Susan's never seen a man naked before and she's very nervous. Tony takes his shirt off and reveals his broad hairy chest. Susan runs downstairs and says, "Mom! Tony has hair all over his chest. Is that normal?" "Of course it is," replies mother. "I like a man with a hairy chest." Susan goes back upstairs and sees Tony taking off his trousers. She runs downstairs and says, "Mom! Tony has a tight little ass. Is that normal?" "Yes," replies mother. "I like a man with a small butt."

Susan goes upstairs and finds Tony completely naked. She rushes downstairs again. "Mom! Mom! I just saw Tony's thingy – it's over a foot long! Is that normal?" Mom shakes her head. "No it isn't, dear," she says. "That's not normal at all. You stay down here – this sounds like a job for mommy."

Teacher says, "Children, if you could have one element in the world, what would it be?" Little Jimmy says, "I'd want gold. Then I could buy a Porsche." Little Billy says, "I'd want platinum. Platinum is worth more than gold. I could buy a Porsche and a Ferrari." Little Suzie says, "I want some silicone." "Silicone?" says teacher. "That's not very valuable." "That's what you think," says Little Suzie. "My mommy's got two bags of the stuff and you should see all the sports cars outside our house!"

sharp tongue action

Can I buy you a drink? What are you having?

This minute? An attack of nausea!

I know a fantastic way to burn off some calories.

Me too. It involves running the hell away from you.

So tell me, how did a creep like you beat 1,000,000 other sperm?

Some men are arrogant and rude. But you're completely the opposite – you're rude and arrogant!

If ignorance is bliss, you must be in the middle of one long orgasm.

Do you kiss with your eyes closed?
With you I would.

A hard-on doesn't count as personal growth.

I'd go to the ends of the earth for you.
I'm sure you would – but would you stay there?"

Come on, don't be shy. Ask me out.

Sure. Get out!

Let's be honest, we both came to this bar for the same reason.

Really? You're here to pick up chicks too?

Why don't you come back to my place for some heavy breathing?

Why, is your elevator out of order?

Try all you like, but you'll never be the man your mother was!

So how do you like your eggs in the morning?

Unfertilized!

I like the way you dye the roots of your hair brown.

Yeah? Well at least I've got some roots.

I bet I know what you use for contraception – your personality.

I thought I saw a description of you on a loaf of bread this morning. But when I looked again it actually said, "Thick cut."

Baby, I'd go through anything for you.
Fantastic! Let's start with your savings account!

Do you know the best way to practice safe sex?
Go screw yourself!

I'd like to see things from your point of view, but
I could never get my head so far up my ass.

If I'd known I was going to run into a girl as beautiful as you, I'd have plucked my nostrils.

And if I'd known I was going to meet someone looking like you, I'd have plucked my eyeballs.

If you kiss me, I promise I won't turn into a frog.

So why would I want to kiss you?

It was fantastic meeting you tonight. Why don't we do it again?

Because I'd rather die.

I've got a couple of movie tickets. Want to go?

Sure, but only if I get both of them.

My ideal woman has to have a great sense of humor.

Looking at you – she'd need one!

So what does a sweet thing like you do for a living?

I'm a female impersonator.

If I asked you to marry me, what would you say?

Nothing. I get the hiccups when I try to talk and laugh at the same time.

What's it like being the best-looking person in the room?

You'll never know.

Put a sock in it! A man with your IQ should have a low voice too!

Your figure is turning a few heads.

And your face is turning a few stomachs.

Are you trying to imagine me naked?

No. I'm trying to imagine you with a personality.

Are these your eyeballs? I just found them in my cleavage.

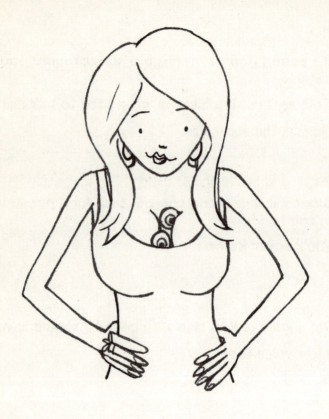

Every man has the right to be ugly, but don't abuse the privilege!

You're as much use as a condom vending machine in the Vatican!

When shall we meet up again?
How about never? Is never good for you?

I'd love to go out with you tonight, but I'm really busy – my favorite baked bean commercial might be on TV this evening.

Do you know what – we'd all be a lot happier if your dad had settled for a blowjob.

each to their own devices

I'm better at sex than anyone I know. Now all I need is a partner.

A man goes to a brothel and says to the madam, "What can I get for five dollars?" "Five dollars!" says the madam. "You can take a hike and get yourself off." The man leaves. A few minutes later, he comes back and says, "Who do I give the fiver to?"

A woman goes to her doctor for a checkup. The doctor examines her and finds a large lump of pink wax in her navel. "How did that get there?" he asks. "Well, it's sort of embarrassing," says the woman. "But my boyfriend likes to eat by candlelight..."

Why did early men learn to walk upright?
To leave their hands free for beating off.

After a visit to a massage parlor, a man finds a painful lump on his dick. He goes to see a doctor. The doctor does a thorough examination, then says, "I'm afraid this is serious. You know how boxers can get a cauliflower ear?" "Yes," says the man. The doctor replies, "Well you've got a brothel sprout."

A man wins a camel in a bet and rides it home. "What the hell is that thing?" asks his wife. "It's a male camel," says her husband. "How can you tell it's a male?" she asks. "You don't know anything about camels." "It must be a male," replies the man. "On the way here at least ten people pointed at us and shouted 'Hey – look at the dick on that camel!'"

A man is in the bedroom admiring his dick. He turns to his wife and says, "You know what – two inches more, and I'd be king." She looks at it and says, "Two inches less, and you'd be queen."

Tracy decides to surprise her boyfriend and buys a pair of crotchless panties. She's lying on the bed when her boyfriend comes in. Tracy spreads her legs and says, "Hey, big boy. Do you want some of this?" "Christ no!" shrieks her boyfriend. "Look what it's done to your panties!"

A guy walks into a bar looking miserable. "What's up?" asks the bartender. "I've just discovered my oldest son is gay," replies the man. A week later, the man comes back looking even more depressed. He says to the bartender, "I've just discovered my second son is gay as well." A week later he's back again, looking suicidal. "This morning my youngest son told me he's gay too," says the man. "Jeez," says the bartender. "So does anyone in your family like women?" "Yeah," sighs the man. "It turns out my wife does."

If you mix Viagra and Prozac you end up with a guy who's ready to go, but doesn't really care where.

A little old man walks into a pharmacy to buy Viagra. "Can I have six tablets, please," he says. "And I need them cut into quarters." "I could cut them up," says the pharmacist. "But a quarter of a tablet won't give you a full erection." "I'm 96," says the old man. "I don't have much use for an erection. I just want it sticking out far enough so I don't piss on my slippers."

An old lady staggers into a sex shop. She hobbles to the counter and grabs it for support. "D-d-do y-y-yo-o-u s-s-s-ell v-v-v-vibr-br-rators?" she says. "Sure," replies the sales clerk. "We've got lots of them." The old lady gasps, "D-d-d-do y-y-you ha-have a-a-a-a b-b-big r-r-red o-o-one, e-e-eight i-i-i-inches l-l-long c-c-c-alled Th-th-the P-p-p-punish-sh-sher?" The clerk replies, "Yeah, we do sell that one." "I-i-in th-th-that c-ca-case," says the little old lady, "C-c-could y-y-ou t-t-tell m-m-me h-how t-to t-t-tturn th-th-the fu-fu-fucking th-th-th-thing o-o-off?"

A father finds his son in the shed banging a nail into the wall. "That's a big nail," says father. "It's not a nail," says the boy. "It's a worm. I mixed some stuff together from my chemistry set, dipped this worm in it and it became as hard as steel." Father is impressed. "Tell you what," he says. "Give me your formula and I'll buy you a car." The boy agrees and the next day he and his dad go and look in the garage. Parked inside are a second-hand Volkswagen and a brand new Ferrari. "Wow," says the boy. "Which one's mine." "Both," replies father. "I got you the Volkswagen. The Ferrari's from your mother."

A woman goes to the doctor's with a vibrator jammed up her pussy. "Get on the examination table," says the doctor. "I'll have it out in a minute."

"Get it out?" says the woman. "I don't want it out. I want you to change the batteries!"

Two couples decide to spice up their sex live by swapping partners. Later that night, one of the guys rolls over in bed and says, "Hey. I wonder what our wives are up to?"

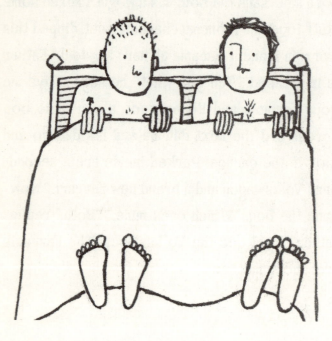

A woman goes to her doctor with a problem – her husband isn't interested in sex any more and she wants the doctor to give her some Viagra. The doctor gives her a small bottle of tablets. "These are new," he says. "They're very powerful and they may have side effects we don't know about. Whatever happens, your husband must not take more than one a month!" The woman goes home, but she's too embarrassed to ask her husband to take a pill so she decides to slip him a tablet in his cup of coffee. She makes him a cup, but drops in two tablets by mistake. The woman doesn't want to waste the pills so she stirs them in, drinks half the coffee herself and gives the rest to her husband in the next room. She thinks it might take an hour or two for the tablet to work, but seconds later, her husband storms into the room looking wild-eyed. He tears off his sweat-soaked shirt and shouts "I want a woman! I want a woman right now!!" The woman gulps and wipes a bead of sweat from her forehead. "You know what?" she gulps. "I think I want one too."

Sandra comes home early from work. She goes into the living room, and finds her naked husband kneeling on the carpet having sex with the reverend's wife doggy-style. "You bastard!" she yells. "I knew you were seeing other women, but this time you've gone too far!" "You're right," moans hubby. "I think I'm stuck."

My boyfriend wanted to be an unstoppable sex machine, but he failed the practicum.

Suzanne is telling her friend Jane about a sex game she plays with her boyfriend. "We get naked and sit opposite each other on the floor," she says. "Then my boyfriend throws grapes at my pussy and I throw doughnuts over his dick. If he gets a grape in my pussy, he eats it; and if I get a doughnut over his erection, I get to eat that." "I'm going to try that with my boyfriend," says Jane. "D'you think the corner shop will still be open?" "It might be," says Suzanne. "But I don't think they sell doughnuts or grapes." "I don't need doughnuts or grapes," says Jane. "I need a box of Cheerios and a sack of apples."

chapter 7

intimate problems

A couple visits a sex counselor to see if they can improve their love life. "Have you thought about different positions?" asks the counselor. "How about the Wheelbarrow? Your wife gets on her hands and knees, you stand behind her, lift up her legs, get inside her, and off you go!" When they get home the husband asks his wife if she want to try the Wheelbarrow. "Well, okay," she says. "But on two conditions. First, if it hurts, you'll stop straight away. And second, you have to promise we won't go past my mother's house."

Do you know that they've started giving Viagra to old men in nursing homes?
Apparently it keeps them from rolling out of bed!

Two elderly widows are discussing their dead husbands. "Did you have mutual orgasms?" asks one. "No," says the other. "I think we were with the Prudential."

A woman goes to her doctor and explains that her husband is impotent. The doctor writes her a prescription. "This is strong stuff," he says. "Get this tonic and put three drops in his milk before he goes to bed. No more than that." Two weeks later, the woman comes back. "So how's your husband?" asks the doctor. "He's dead," sniffs the women. "One night I put thirty drops in his milk by accident – I came back for an antidote so we can shut the lid on his coffin."

After God had created Adam he noticed that he looked very lonely. He said "Adam, I've decided to make you a woman. She'll love you, cook for you, clean for you, and be sweet to you." Adam said, "Fantastic! How much will she cost me?" God answered, "An arm and a leg." "Well," said Adam, "in that case, what can I get for a rib?"

A woman goes into an adult shop to buy a dildo. The guy behind the counter shows her the best dildo they have – the Magic Dildo. "The Magic Dildo will do whatever you want," says the guy. "Just say 'Magic Dildo my ... something' it starts screwing you there." Impressed, the woman buys one and leaves. While she's driving home the woman decides to try it out. "Magic Dildo my shoulder!" says the woman. The dildo jumps out of its box and it starts buzzing over her shoulder and neck. Then the woman says, "Magic Dildo my pussy!" and the dildo jumps under her skirt and starts screwing her. Not surprisingly, the woman loses control of the car starts swerving over the road. A policeman pulls her over. "I'm so sorry, officer," says the woman. "It's this dildo I just bought. It's a Magic Dildo and it took me by surprise." The policeman thought he'd heard every excuse there is, but this one has to be the craziest. "Yeah, right," he snorts. "Magic dildo my ass!"

A prospector goes to a remote mining town and is horrified to find that the locals use sheep for sex – they have to, there's not a woman for a hundred miles. The man resists temptation for as long as he can, but one night he can't stand it any more. He goes out, finds a pretty young sheep in a field, and takes her home to bed. The next day, the man takes a walk into town with his new lady friend and visits the saloon. The man walks into the bar with the sheep, and the place goes silent – everyone stares at him in horror. "What's the matter?" says the man. "Don't pretend to be shocked. You all sleep with sheep too." "Well, sure we do," replies the bartender. "But never with the preacher's wife!"

A mother is cleaning her teenage daughter's room when she finds a bondage magazine hidden under her bed. She shows the magazine to her husband. "What do you think we should do?" asks the woman. Her husband flicks through the magazine and says, "Well, I don't think spanking her is going to help."

A number of flights are canceled due to bad weather and the airport hotel fills up. It gets so overcrowded that people have to share rooms, and three men find themselves sleeping in the same bed. The next morning the man on the right-hand side of the bed says, "I had a great dream. I dreamt that a beautiful woman was jerking me off all night." "That's a coincidence," says the man on the left-hand side of the bed, "I had exactly the same dream – someone was giving me a hand job all night long." "What a couple of perverts," says the man in the middle. "I had a very nice dream – all about skiing."

Father O'Leary is rubbing one out in the cathedral vestry when a tourist sees him and takes his picture. "Oh my God!" says Father O'Leary. "I'll be ruined. How much d'you want for that camera?" "Six hundred dollars," says the tourist. Father O'Leary ducks over to the bank with the tourist, pays him the money, then takes the camera back to the vestry. Sister Sarah comes by. "That's a very nice camera, Father," she says. "How much was it?" "Six hundred dollars," replies Father O'Leary.

"Christ!" exclaims the Sister. "Someone must've seen you coming!"

Jumbo the elephant has no interest in sex and refuses to mate with any of the female elephants in the zoo. His keeper calls in an animal sex expert who suggests that the keeper arouses Jumbo by stroking his dick with a long wooden pole. A few weeks later the expert phones the zoo to see if Jumbo has started mating. "No," said the zookeeper. "Stroking him with a stick did give him a hard-on, but now we can't get him away from the TV when a pool tournament comes on."

A man joins the military and is posted to a remote fort in the desert. When he gets there, the sergeant explains that there are no women for miles and the men rely on camels for sex. That evening, a herd of camels is released onto the fort's parade ground and the men go wild, chasing them all over the place. The new recruit watches with disgust. The sergeant sees him and comes over. "What are you waiting for?" he says. "What's the hurry?" replies the new recruit. "There must be over a hundred camels running around." "Well, suit yourself," says the sergeant. "But don't blame me if you get stuck with an ugly one."

A woman is crying on a park bench. An old man comes by and asks her what's the matter. "My husband was caught having sex with one of his patients," she sobs. "He's been cheating on me and now it looks like he'll be laid off." "That's terrible," says the old man. "But look on the bright side – news like that can't get any worse." "Oh yes it can," sobs the women. "He's a vet!"

Two firemen are having sex in a smoke-filled room. The fire chief bursts in and sees them. "What the hell is going on?" he shouts. One of the firemen looks up and says, "Jones is suffering from smoke inhalation, sir!" The chief says, "Well why aren't you giving him mouth-to-mouth resuscitation?" "I did, sir," replies the fireman. "How the hell d'you think all this got started?!"

When you're on the beach, how can you recognize a guy who uses an inflatable sex doll? He's the one who ignores the bikinis and stares at the beach balls!

A man falls asleep on a beach and gets a really bad sunburn. His wife takes him to hospital and watches as a doctor covers him from head to foot in skin cream. Then the doctor gives the man some Viagra. "Viagra?" says the wife. "What good will

Viagra do in his condition?" "Not much," says the doctor. "But it'll help keep the sheets off him."

An old lady walks into a psychiatrist's office. "Doctor," she says. "I think I might be a nymphomaniac." "I can help you," replies the psychiatrist. "But I'm expensive: I charge $100 an hour." "That's not bad," replies the old lady. "But how much for the whole night?"

A man goes into a public toilet and sees a man with no arms standing by the urinal. The armless man turns to him and says, "Could you help me, please? My zipper needs undoing." "Okay," says the first man, and he pulls down the man's zipper. The armless man then says, "Could you take it out for me?" "Um, well, okay," says the first man. He pulls the armless man's dick out of his pants and sees that it's covered in red bumps, green veins and brown scabs oozing with yellow goo. It really stinks too! "Could you point it for me?" asks the armless man. The other man tries to hold the horrible dick steady while the armless man has a pee. When he's finished, the armless man says, "Now could you put it back in?" "Sure," says the first man. He shakes the putrid dick dry, stuffs it back in the armless man's trousers and zips up his fly. "Thank you," says the armless man. "I really appreciate that." "No problem," says the first man. "But I've got to ask you something – what the hell is wrong with your dick?" The other guy pulls his arms out of his jacket and says, "Damned if I know, but I sure ain't touching it … "

They now have a thing called "Marriage Anonymous." If you ever feel like getting married, you call them up and they send over an unshaven man in a dirty T-shirt who'll sit in front of your TV for three days farting, drinking beer and asking for the occasional blowjob.

An old lady goes into a sex shop. She asks to see the dildos and the sales clerk shows her a display cabinet full of them. After having a good look, the old lady goes back to the counter. "Could I have the 14-inch Ramrod in black," she says. "And the 24-inch double-ended one in pink, and the big red one on the wall." "Well I can get you the first two," says the clerk. "But the last one has to stay where it is – that's the fire extinguisher."

A woman goes into a coma after a car crash. One day, a hospital doctor rings the woman's husband and tells him there's been a change in her condition – when the nurses wash her, they've noticed a response when they touch her breasts. The doctor suggests that the husband visits his wife and tries rubbing her breasts himself. The husband does so and there are definite signs of awareness. Next, the doctor suggests that the man massages his wife's privates. The husband does so and the response is even greater – it looks like she might be waking up! Finally the doctor suggests something even more stimulating – oral sex. The man goes into his wife's room, but a couple of minutes later her heart monitor starts beeping like crazy. The doctor runs in to help. "My God!" he says. "What happened?" "I don't know," replies her husband. "I think she choked!"

A female dwarf goes to a doctor – her pussy is really sore and she has no idea why. The doctor tells her to lie down and lift up her skirt so he can examine her. A moment later he picks up a pair of scissors and starts snipping away at something. When he's finished he tells the dwarf to stand up, walk around, and see if she feels any better. "That's much better," says the dwarf. "My pussy's not sore at all now. What did you do?" The doctor replies, "I trimmed the top off your boots."

A woman is about to have an operation. She's laid on a hospital bed and wheeled into the hallway. The nurse leaves her outside the operating room and goes to tell the surgeon she's ready. A man in a white coat comes by, lifts up the woman's sheet and peers at her naked body. He then calls over to another man in a white coat who comes over and has a look as well. "Is something the matter?" asks the woman. "I wouldn't know," says the first man. "We're just here to paint the ceiling."

Women's Problems

MEN-strual cramps

MEN-opause

GUY-nacologist

And if things get really bad, a...HIS-terectomy.

Can it really be a coincidence that all women's problems start with men?!

A doctor tells a female patient that her pussy is almost burnt out from too much sex – she can only use it another 30 times before it will collapse.

The woman goes home and tells her husband the news. "That's terrible," he says. "With so few left we can't waste any – let's make a list of special occasions." "Sorry," says the woman. "I already made a list – you're not on it."

A man suffering from premature ejaculation goes to see his doctor. As a cure, the doctor suggests that the man tries to startle himself when he's about to come – something that makes a loud noise should do it. The man goes home, but returns the next day with a bandage round his dick. "What happened?" asks the doctor. "Well, doc," says the man. "I bought a starter pistol to make a loud noise. Then I ran home and found my wife naked in the bedroom. We got straight to it and started sixty-nining. I felt myself coming so I fired the gun. Then my wife crapped on my head, bit two inches off my dick, and my neighbor jumped out of the wardrobe with his hands in the air."

A man discovers that his dick has gone green and goes to a doctor. "I'm sorry," says the doctor. "I can't cure it. We're going to have to amputate." The man is horrified and goes to get a second opinion. "I'm sorry," says the second doctor. "But your dick has got to come off." The man won't accept this, so he seeks a third opinion. "I've got good news and bad news," says the third doctor. "The good news is that we don't have to cut your dick off." "What a relief," says the man, "So what's the bad news?" The doctor replies, "It just fell on the floor."

A woman with a mild hormone imbalance is put on a course of testosterone tablets. A week later she comes back to her doctor for a checkup. "Since I've been taking the pills, I've noticed some extra hair growth," says the woman. "That's not unusual," says the doctor. "Where are you growing this hair?" The woman replies, "On my balls."

A woman with sore knees goes to see her doctor. "It might be my sex life," says the woman. "My boyfriend and I make love four times a week and we always do it 'doggy style.'" "There are other positions," says the doctor. "Yes," says the woman. "But not if you want to watch 'American Idol' as well."

A man is lying in a hospital bed with an oxygen mask over his face. A nurse arrives to sponge him down. "Nurse," mumbles the man, "are my testicles black?" "I don't know," replies the nurse. "I'm only here to wash you." The man says, "But, nurse, are my testicles black?" "I really don't know," says the nurse. Again, the man asks, "Nurse, can you tell me if my testicles are black?" The nurse gives in. She lifts up the man's gown, picks up his dick and takes a good look at his balls. "No," she says. "They're pink." The man pulls off his oxygen mask and says, "Thanks, but are my test results back!?"

Two men get talking in a doctor's waiting room. "Why are you here?" asks one. "I have a red ring around my dick," replies the other. "How about you?" The first man says, "I've got a green ring round my dick." The doctor then calls in the man with the red ring. After a few minutes the man walks out with a relieved look on his face – the doctor's told him he's going to be fine. Then it's the turn of the man with the green ring. The man goes into the doctor's office and drops his trousers. "Bad news," says the doctor. "Your penis is about to drop off." "What?!" says the man. "You told the guy with the red ring that he was going to be okay!" "Yes," replies the doctor. "But there's a big difference between lipstick and gangrene."

girls on top

A man and a woman have an argument about who enjoys sex more; men or women. The man says, "Men must enjoy sex more – we spend all our time trying to get laid." "That doesn't prove anything," says the woman. "When your ear itches and you wiggle your finger in it, which feels better – your ear or your finger?"

In the early hours of the morning, a cop sees a car weaving over the road. He pulls it over and finds a young woman at the wheel, stinking of booze.

The cop asks her to blow in a Breathalyzer and looks at the indicator strip. "I thought so," he says. "It looks like you've had four or five stiff ones tonight." "You're kidding?" says the woman. "You mean it can tell that too?"

A marketing researcher stops three women in the street and asks them how they know if they've had a good night out. The first woman says, "If I come home, get undressed, climb into bed and lay there tingling all over, I know I've had a good night out." The second one says, "If I come home, get undressed, climb into bed and feel like I'm riding a roller-coaster, I know I've had a good night out." The third says, "I come home, get undressed, and throw my panties at the wall; if they stick I know I've had a damn good night out!"

A man is downing a glass of champagne in a bar when he sees a woman doing the same. "Are you celebrating?" he asks. "Yes," replies the woman. "I thought I was infertile, but my doctor just told me I'm pregnant." "Congratulations," says the man. "I'm celebrating too. I'm a chicken farmer and my hens haven't been laying for months. But I eventually figured out what was wrong – I changed cocks." "That's a coincidence," says the woman. "Me too!"

A woman runs into her house and finds her husband in the living room, "Pack your bags!" she says. "I just won the lottery!" "Fantastic!" says the husband. "What should I pack? Where are we going?" "Go where you like," replies the woman, "just hurry and get the fuck out of here!"

Two friends go for a girls' night out on the town. They get really drunk and on the way home they duck into a cemetery for a pee. Once they've finished, one woman wipes herself dry on her panties and throws them away, while the other woman wipes herself with a piece of paper she finds pinned to a wreath. The following morning their boyfriends are comparing notes. One says, "I think we need to start keeping a closer eye on those two. Mine came home last night without any underwear!" The other says, "You think that's bad. When my girlfriend came home she had a card stuck to her pussy saying, 'We will never forget you.'"

An elderly couple get married. On their honeymoon, the husband takes off his glasses and goes to clean his teeth, while his bride does some yoga. She gets naked and does a stretching exercise on the bed, lying on her back and lifting her legs up and over her head. Unfortunately her feet get stuck in the headboard. She calls for help and her husband dashes in. He peers at her and says, "For Christ's sake, Mavis. Brush your hair and put your teeth in. You look just like your mother!"

Two girlfriends are talking. One says, "That dude I picked up last night turned out to be a fucking bastard. After we'd had sex, he called me a slut!" "No way!" says her friend. "What did you do?" The first girl replies, "I told him to get out of my bed and take his nasty friends with him."

Three hillbilly gals are sitting in a bar, chewing the fat. One says, "If ma husband were a soda pop, I'd call him '7-Up.' Because he's got seven inches and it's always up!" The second gal says, "Well if mine was a soda pop, I'd call him 'Mountain Dew' because he can 'mount and dew' me anytime!" The third says, "Well I'd call mine 'Southern Comfort.'" "Southern Comfort?" says the first gal. "That's no soda pop, that's a hard liquor." The third woman replies, "Yup, that's him alright!"

A man goes into a magic shop and sees a pair of "nudie" glasses for sale. "What do they do?" asks the man. "They let you see everyone in the nude," says the storekeeper. "Why not try them on." So the man tries on the glasses and straight-away everyone he looks at is in the nude. The storekeeper is nude, his assistant is nude, even a passerby looking in the window is nude. The man buys the glasses and goes out into the street to look at everyone in the nude. After an hour of fun he decides to sneak home and surprise his wife with his new toy. He gets back, creeps in the living room, and finds his wife and his neighbor nude on the couch. "Surprise!" he shouts, coming into the room. "What do you think of my new glasses?" He takes them off and is surprised to see that his wife and neighbor are still naked. "Damn!" he says. "I've only had them an hour and they're broken already!"

Woman, to man: "You want sex?"

Man: "Your place or mine?"

Woman: "Well if you're going to argue – forget it!"

Why do men find it hard to make eye contact?
Because breasts don't have eyes.

Two midgets pick up a couple of girls and take them back to their hotel. The first midget is unable to get a hard-on, and hearing his friend in the next room doesn't make him feel any better – all night long, all he hears through the wall is his friend shouting, "One, two, three ... Uuuhh!! One, two, three ... Uuuhh!!" The next morning, the midgets compare notes. The first midget says, "It was really embarrassing. I tried everything but I couldn't get an erection." "You think that's embarrassing?" says the second midget. "I couldn't even get up on the bed!"

A woman sees a plastic surgeon about the bags under her eyes. The surgeon removes the bags then puts a small crank in the back of the woman's head. He tells her to turn the crank if she notices any new bags forming – this will tighten up the skin and the bags will disappear. This technique works for many years, but one day an enormous pair of bags appear under the woman's eyes, and no amount of cranking will get rid of them. The surgeon examines her and says, "No wonder you can't get rid of those bags – they're your breasts. You've been turning that crank much too hard." "Oh dear," says the woman. "And I suppose that would also explain the goatee."

What does a 75-year-old woman have between her boobs that a 25-year-old doesn't?
Her navel.

A woman is standing at a bus stop when it starts to rain. The man next to her is smoking a cigarette and as the first drops fall, he takes a condom out of his pocket, snips off the end, and slips it over his cigarette to keep it dry. The woman is a smoker too. She thinks this is a great idea and hurries over to a pharmacy. "Can I have a packet of condoms," she says. "Certainly, madam," says the pharmacist. "What size?" The woman replies, "One that will fit a Camel."

A guy hooks up with a girl in a bar and they end up back at her place. After a night of non-stop fucking the guy gets up and takes a shower. As he's drying off, he sees a photo of a man on the girl's dressing table. The man looks like a nasty piece of work, a real bad-ass, and the guy starts to worry. "Who's that a picture of?" asks the guy. "It's not your husband, or a boyfriend, is it?" "Nah," replies the girl. "That's me before the operation."

A researcher asks a woman if she'd like to do some market research on condoms. "It depends," says the woman. "What's in it for me?"

A couple are relaxing after having sex. The woman says, "If I got pregnant, what would we call the baby?" The man pulls off his condom, ties a knot in it, and flushes it down the toilet. "Well," he says. "If he can get out of that, let's call him Houdini."

Don't believe them when they tell you condoms are safe – a friend of mine was wearing one and he got hit by a bus.

Did you hear about the new "morning after" pill for men?

It changes their DNA.

Have you heard about the new super-sensitive condoms?

After the man leaves they hang around and talk.

Wear camouflage condoms – they won't see you coming.

What's a married man's definition of safe sex?
Meeting his girlfriend at least 50 miles from his house.

A man goes into a pharmacy to buy some condoms. He's confused by the shelves and shelves of condoms on display, and calls over a sales assistant to help. "What size?" asks the sales assistant. "I'm not sure," replies the man. So the assistant sticks her hand down the guy's pants and has a feel. "Medium," she says and hands him a packet of condoms. A second man comes by and asks for help too. He doesn't know his size either so the assistant has a feel down his pants. "Medium," she says and hands him a packet of condoms. Next a schoolboy comes up to her. "What do you want?" asks the assistant. "Condoms," says the boy. "What size?" asks the assistant. "Don't know," says the boy. So the assistant puts her hand down his pants and has a rummage. Then she leans over to a microphone, presses the button and says, "Clean up in aisle five! Clean up in aisle five!"

Mary and Patrick practice the "stool and saucer" method of contraception. Patrick (who is 5 feet 5 inches tall) and Mary (6 feet 3 inches tall) make love upright, with Patrick standing on a stool and Mary leaning against a wall. When his eyes get as big as saucers – she kicks away the stool.

Good: Your boyfriend likes to keep the lights on while he's having sex.

Bad: He also likes to keep the curtains wide open.

Ugly: You first notice this while waiting at the bus stop opposite his house!

Good: Your boyfriend likes showing you off to his friends.

Bad: He secretly films you doing a striptease.

Ugly: It brings the house down on "America's Funniest Home Videos"!

Good: Your boyfriend has an 18-inch tongue.

Bad: He has to be in the next room to go down on you.

Ugly: He keeps breaking off to catch flies!

Good: Your boyfriend finally cleans out his bedroom.

Bad: You find a pile of old porno tapes in his bin.

Ugly: Your mother is starring in most of them!

Good: Your boyfriend gets on well with your parents.

Bad: He says he has more in common with your mom than you.

Ugly: He elopes with your dad!

Good: Your boyfriend is concerned about your health.

Bad: He tells you he might have given you the clap.

Ugly: He thinks he caught it off a goat!

Good: You can't find your vibrator anywhere.

Bad: You suspect your husband has been messing around with it.

Ugly: You hear a humming sound whenever he bends over!

Good: Your friend sets you up with a blind date.

Bad: He's short, bald and morbidly obese.

Ugly: He won't return your calls!

Good: The recruitment agency finds you a job.

Bad: They send you to a sleazy strip club.

Ugly: You're their new cleaning lady!

Good: You give the birds and bees speech to your 14-year-old daughter.

Bad: She keeps interrupting you.

Ugly: With corrections!

Good: Your boyfriend enjoys going clothes shopping with you.

Bad: You catch him wearing your new dress.

Ugly: He looks better in it than you do!

let's get it on

A man goes to his doctor and says, "I got this problem. My wife always wakes me up at 1 a.m. for sex, and then at 5 a.m. so we can do it again before I go to work." "I see ... " says the doctor. "There's more," says the man. "When I get on the train I meet this girl every day. We get a compartment to ourselves and screw all the way into town. Then, when I get to the office I usually give my secretary one in the storeroom." "I see ... " says the doctor. "No. There's more," says the man. "When I go to lunch I always meet up with this waitress and we slip into a back alley for a half-hour fuck." "Now I understand ... " says the doctor. "No. There's more," says the man. "When I get back to the office I have to spend the afternoon having sex with my boss. She says she'll fire me if I don't." "Ahh ... " says the doctor. "Now I see ... " "No. There's more," says the man. "When I get home, my wife gives me a blowjob before dinner, another one afterwards and then we have sex till midnight." "I see," says the doctor. "Have you finished now?" "Yes," says the man. "So what exactly is your problem?" asks the doctor. "Well, y'see doc ... " says the man. "It hurts when I masturbate ... "

A woman goes to see her doctor. "Every time my husband climaxes in bed, he lets out this ear-splitting yell," she says. "Well that's quite natural," replies the doctor. "What's the problem?" The woman replies, "The problem is, it wakes me up."

A doctor is having sex with one of his female patients. Suddenly her husband bursts into the room holding a shotgun. The doctor panics. "It's not what it looks like!" he shouts. "I was only taking her temperature!" "Oh yeah?" says the husband aiming his gun at the doctor's crotch. "Then you'd better hope it's got some numbers on it when you take it out!"

A little girl goes up to her mother and says, "Mom, every night I hear you and Daddy making 'noises.' And when I look in your room you're bouncing up and down on him." Mother thinks quickly and says, "I bounce on your Father's tummy like that because he's fat and it makes him thin again." "Well that's not going to work," says the girl. "Why not?" asks Mom. The girl replies, "Because the lady next door comes by every afternoon and blows him back up again!"

A little girl goes up to her dad and says, "Daddy when my cat died, why did it lie on its back with its legs in the air?" Daddy replies, "Well its legs were up like that to make it easier for Jesus to grab him and pull him up to heaven." "Wow," says the girl. "That means Mommy almost died this morning!" "What d'you mean?" asks Dad. The girl replies,

"After you'd gone to work, I looked into Mommy's room. She was lying on the bed with her legs in the air shouting 'Jesus! I'm coming!' and if it hadn't have been for the milkman holding her down, he would have got her!"

A man takes early retirement and buys a remote cottage in the Scottish Highlands. One day, he hears a knock on the door and finds a huge, bearded Scottish farmer standing outside. "I hear you're new here," says the farmer. "That's right," replies the man. "Then I'd like to invite you to a party I'm having," says the farmer. "Thank you," says the man. "I'd love to come." "I warn you though, there'll be lots of drinking," says the farmer. "I like a drink," replies the man. "And there might be a bit of rough stuff too," says the farmer. "That's okay," says the man. "I can take care of myself." "And things might get a bit frisky later on," says the farmer. "There'll be some hanky panky going on, no doubt." "That sounds great," says the man. "I like the ladies." "Och, there'll be no lassies," says the farmer. "It's just the two of us."

Teacher asks her class to say a sentence with the word "beautiful" in it twice. Little Johnny stands up and says, "My dad bought my mom a beautiful new dress and she looked beautiful in it." "Very good, Johnny," says teacher. Then little Michael stands up and says, "Yesterday was a beautiful day and I saw a beautiful flower." "Well done, Michael!" says teacher. She then turns to little Suzie and asks her if she can think of a sentence. Little Suzie thinks for a moment, then says, "Last night my big sister told my dad she was pregnant, and he said, 'Beautiful, fucking beautiful!'"

Two nuns are walking on the beach when they come across some secluded dunes and decide to do some sunbathing. They both strip and lie naked on the sand, soaking up the sunshine. Suddenly one of the nuns realizes they're being spied on by a pervert with a camera. The pervert is hiding behind a bush taking pictures of the naked nuns. However he's so worked up he's not even looking through the viewfinder, he's just snapping away at random. One of the nuns calls out, "Hey! Aren't you going to focus?" The other nun says, "Give him a chance, sister. Let him take his pictures first."

Little Johnny has a brand new watch and little Suzie asks how he got it. "Yesterday I got home early," says Johnny. "And I heard noises coming from Mom and Dad's bedroom. I walked in and saw Dad and the lady from next door bouncing in bed. Dad said I could have anything I wanted if I didn't tell Mommy, so I asked for a watch." Suzie decides she'd like a watch too. That night she listens outside her parents' bedroom and hears some banging and groaning. She walks in and finds her mommy sitting on Daddy. "What do you want?" asks Mommy. Suzie says, "I want a watch." "Well, okay," sighs Mommy. "But stand in the corner and don't make any noise."

An heiress is discussing Christmas presents with her maid. "What present should I get the butler?" she asks. "A bottle of wine?" suggests the maid. The heiress frowns. "He doesn't need that. I'll get him a tie. Now what about the cook?" The maid replies, "What about some perfume?" The heiress tuts, "She doesn't need perfume. I'll get her an apron." "Now," says the heiress. "What about my husband?" The maid says, "I assume you want to get him something he really needs, madam?" "Of course," says the heiress. The maid replies, "Well in that case, how about five more inches?"

A husband comes home and finds his wife in bed with another man. He drags the man into the garage puts the guy's dick in a vice and picks up a hacksaw. The man screams, "For God's sakes don't do it! Don't cut it off!" The husband takes the handle off the vice, gives the man the hacksaw and says, "I'm not going to cut it off. I'm going to set fire to the garage."

A couple is celebrating their silver wedding anniversary when the husband asks his wife if she's ever been unfaithful. "Three times," answers the wife. "Remember when you needed money to start your business? Well I slept with the bank manager to get you a loan." "So that's why he gave me the money," says the astonished husband. His wife continues, "The second time was when I slept with the surgeon who did your heart operation. He was the only one who specialized in your condition and we couldn't afford his fees." "Oh my God," says the husband. "You saved my life. And what was the third time?" "Well," says his wife. "Remember when you wanted to be president of the golf club and you were 42 votes short...?"

A guy goes into a pharmacy to buy condoms. The pharmacist says the condoms come in packs of 3, 9 or 12 and asks which one he wants. "Well," he said, "I've been seeing this girl for a while and I want the condoms because I think tonight's the night. We're having dinner with her parents, and I've got a feeling I'm going to get lucky after that. Once she's had me, she'll want me all the time, so I better have the 12-pack." The guy buys the condoms and leaves. Later that evening, he sits down to dinner with his girlfriend and her parents. He asks if he might give the blessing and begins the prayer, but continues praying for several minutes. The girlfriend whispers to him, "You never told me that you were so religious." The guy whispers back, "You never told me your father is a pharmacist."

Teacher walks into her classroom on Monday and sees that someone had written "dick" on the blackboard. She gives her class a stern look then rubs the word off the board. The same thing happens the next day, except that this time "dick" is written in much larger letters. Again, teacher gives her class a glare and rubs the word off the board. Unfortunately, this goes on all week, and each day the word "dick" gets bigger and bigger. Finally teacher comes into class on Friday and finds "dick" written in huge letters right across the blackboard. Underneath is a note saying, "Dick. The more you rub it the bigger it gets!"

A girl brings her boyfriend home after a night out. The boyfriend is desperate to use the toilet but the girl is afraid he'll wake her parents if he goes upstairs. "Go and use the kitchen sink," she whispers. "No one will know if we rinse it out later." So the boyfriend slips into the kitchen. A few minutes later he sticks his head round the door. "Have you finished?" asks the girl. "Not quite," says the boyfriend. "Have you got any toilet paper?"

Teacher asks her class to talk about a something they think is important. Little Suzie volunteers and walks to the front of the class where she draws a tiny dot on the blackboard. "What's that?" asks teacher. "It's a period," replies Suzie. "Well it's very nice," says Teacher. "But is it important?" "I guess it must be," says Suzie. "This morning my big sister said she'd missed hers, and Daddy had a stroke, Mommy passed out, and the man next door shot himself."

A woman goes to a doctor and tells him that her husband is 300% impotent. "300% impotent!," says the doc. "I'm not sure I understand what you mean." The woman says, "He can't get an erection; last week he broke his fingers; and this morning he burned his tongue!"

A divorce lawyer is speaking to his client, Sandra. "Your husband says you lied to him," says the lawyer. "That's bullshit," says Sandra. "He lied to me. He said he'd be out till midnight, and the bastard came home at 9:30."

A couple is having sex. The woman says, "You don't have AIDS do you?" "No," replies the man. "Thank fuck for that!" says the woman. "I wouldn't like to catch that again!"

Why are married women heavier than single women?

Single women come home, see what's in the fridge and go to bed. Married women come home, see what's in bed and go to the fridge.

A couple is saving up for their vacation and the husband has the idea of putting some money in a cash box every time they have sex. A month later he counts the money and finds over $1000. "Where did all that come from?" asks the husband. "I was only putting in $20 a go." "You might have been," replies his wife. "But not everyone's as stingy as you are!"

A man comes home early from work and finds his wife having sex with a midget from the local circus. "What?!" he cries. "First it was the world's tallest man, then it was a trapeze artist, then the lion tamer, and now it's a midget!" "Oh come on," says his wife. "At least I'm cutting back."

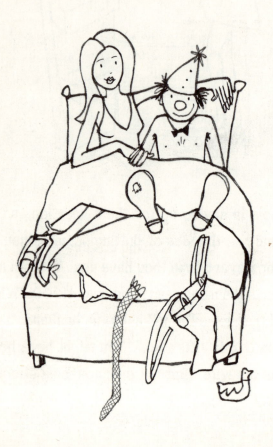

The Sassy Bitch's Book of Dirty Jokes

What a woman says: Come on. This place is a mess! You and I need to clean. Your pants are on the floor and you'll have no clothes if we don't do the laundry now!

What a man hears: Come on...Blah, blah, blah... YOU AND I...blah, blah, blah, blah, blah... ON THE FLOOR...blah, blah, blah...NO CLOTHES...blah, blah, blah, blah...NOW!

Lorenzo, the Italian stallion, walks into a bar looking worried. "Hey, Lorenzo," says the bartender. "Why the long face?" "Some pissed-off husband sent me a letter," says Lorenzo. "He said he'd cut my balls off and make me eat them if I didn't stop screwing his wife." "So why don't you stop?" asks the bartender. "I can't," says Lorenzo. "He didn't sign his name!"

How do you know if elephants have been having sex in your kitchen?

The garbage bags are missing.

A husband thinks his wife is having an affair, so he bursts into their high-rise apartment to catch her in the act. He finds his wife naked on the bed, but can't see a man anywhere. He looks around the flat, then glances out of the window and sees a man running down the stairs. The husband looks around for a missile then picks up the kitchen fridge and lobs it out of the window. The fridge lands on the man as he's running across the parking lot and flattens him. The husband has had his revenge, but the strain of lifting the fridge was too much and he drops dead from a heart attack. A few minutes later, the husband is waiting in line outside the gates into heaven with two other men. One of the men asks him how he died. "I picked up something heavy and had a heart attack," says the husband. "You won't believe what happened to me," says the man. "I was running for a bus when some bastard dropped a heavy weight on me." "That's nothing," says the third man. "I was hiding in this fridge ... "

Psychiatrist, to woman: "When you make
love, do you ever look your husband in
the eyes."

Woman: "Yes, but I only did it once – he looked
very, very angry."

Psychiatrist: "And why do you think
that was?"

Woman: "Because he was looking in through
the bedroom window."

You should always talk to your boyfriend when you're having sex – assuming there's a phone handy.

A woman sneaks up behind her husband and hits him over the head with her shoe. "What the hell was that for!?" shouts the man. "You're having an affair!" says the woman. "There was a piece of paper in your jacket pocket with 'Dirty Sally' written on it and a phone number." "That's the name of a horse!" exclaims the man. "I called a bookie to make a bet." Next day the woman sneaks up again. This time she hits her husband with a golf club. "What is it now!?" cries the man. The woman replies, "Your horse phoned!!"

A girl goes up to her boyfriend and says, "Do you want to hear something that will make you happy and sad at exactly the same time?" "Go on," says the boyfriend. "Okay," says the girl. "Your dick is much, much bigger than your brother's."

Boyfriend, to Girl: "Why can't I tell when you have an orgasm?"

Girl: "Because you're never at home when it happens."

A doctor and his wife are arguing about their sex life. It ends with the doctor telling his wife that she's lousy in bed. The doctor goes to work where he calms down and realizes he ought to apologize. He rings home and waits, and waits, and waits for the phone to be picked up. Eventually his wife answers. "What took you so long?" asks the doctor. "Well," says his wife. "Y'know how you said I was lousy in bed." "Yes," says the doctor. The wife replies, "Well I was getting a second opinion!"

Boyfriend, to Girl: "You know, from the first time I ever saw you, I've wanted to make love to you terribly."

Girl: "Well, you've certainly done that ... "

Man: "Doctor, I suffer from premature ejaculation. Can you help me?!"

Doctor: "No, but I can introduce you to a woman with a short attention span!"

A guy says to his friend, "My girlfriend always laughs during sex. It doesn't matter what she's reading."

A man and a woman get together in a bar. At the end of the night the pair end up having sex in the back of the man's car. The woman is insatiable – she wants more and more. Eventually the man staggers out for a break and sees a man changing the tire on his truck. The man goes over and says, "I've got a really hot date in my car, but I need a rest. Will you go in there and have sex with her till I've recovered – it's so dark she won't know the difference." The second man agrees and climbs into the back of the car, which soon starts to rock rhythmically. A policeman walks by. He shines a flashlight in the back of the car and says, "What's going on in here?" The man replies, "I'm having sex with my wife." "Couldn't you do that in home?" asks the policeman. "I could," replies the man. "But until you shone that flashlight in her face I didn't realize it was my wife."

A young couple have sex for the first time. It's over in a flash. The boy says, "If I'd known you were a virgin, I would have taken more time." His girlfriend says, "If I'd had more time, I would have taken off my tights!"

One morning, a man walks into the kitchen and finds his wife cooking breakfast in her bathrobe. She turns to him and says, "Don't say a word. Screw me right now, here on the table!" She whips off her robe, lies back on the kitchen table and her husband makes passionate love to her. When they've finished, the man says, "That was fantastic. But what's the occasion? Is it your birthday?" "No," says his wife. "I'm boiling an egg and the timer is broken."

An impotent man goes to a witch doctor for help. The witch doctor casts a spell, then tells the man to say "One, two, three" if he wants an erection. The erection will then stay rock-hard until someone says "One, two, three, four," at which point the erection will shrivel away. There's a catch however, the spell can only be used once a year. The man is delighted. He rushes home, jumps into bed with his wife, and shouts "One, two, three." Puzzled, his wife says, "Why did you say 'One, two, three' for'?"

Why do so many men suffer from premature ejaculation?

Because they have to rush back to the bar to tell their buddies what they've been up to.

Did you hear about the idiot who filled his condom with ice?

He wanted to keep the swelling down!

A couple have sex for the first time. After it's over, the girl tells the guy he was lousy in bed. "What d'you mean 'lousy'? he says. "How can you have any sort of opinion after only 15 seconds?"

One day a woman discovers that her husband is impotent – in fact, all their married life he's been using a strap-on dildo. "That's awful," says his wife. "How could you lie to me like that?" "I'm sorry, honey," replies her husband. "But, on the other hand, I'd be quite interested to hear you explain our three children."

Last night my boyfriend made love to me for an hour and five minutes – it was the night they switched the clocks forward!

A girl goes to confession. "Father," she says. "Last night my boyfriend made love to me six times." The priest replies, "For this act of fornication, you must go home and suck six lemons." "And will that absolve me,

Father?" asks the girl. "No," says the priest. "But it might wipe that damned grin off your face."

If you're planning on getting married, you might as well go for a younger man – they never mature anyway.

A woman drives her date out into the countryside where they park on an empty road. They start to make out like crazy, but suddenly the guy says, "Look, I should have mentioned this earlier – but I'm actually a gigolo. I charge $200 for sex." The woman is stunned, but the guy is gorgeous so she pays him and they fuck each other's brains out. After they've finished, the guy asks to be driven home. The woman asks for her fare. "What d'you mean, fare?" says the guy. "Well, I should have mentioned this earlier," replies the woman. "But I'm actually a taxi driver. The fare back to town is $200!"

A woman phones her doctor in the middle of the night. "Doctor! Doctor! Come quickly," she says. "My son has just swallowed a condom!" The doctor gets out of bed and starts pulling on his clothes. The phone rings again – it's the woman. "It's okay," she says. "You don't have to come after all. My husband's just found another one."

It's a summer night and a couple are out fucking in the backyard. The guy is giving his girlfriend oral sex. "I'd love to be able to see this," he says. "I wish I'd bought a flashlight" "So do I," replies the girl. "For the last five minutes you've been eating grass!"

A man goes into a store to buy some condoms. He sees a new brand of multisize condoms, but isn't sure what size will fit him. He asks the girl serving behind the counter for some help. "Are you that big?" asks the girl, holding up one finger. "I'm bigger than that," says the man. The girl holds up two fingers. "Are you that big?" she asks. "Bigger," replies the man. The girl holds up three fingers. "Are you that big?" she asks. "Well, yes," says the man. "I suppose so." The girl sticks the three fingers in her mouth and wiggles them around for a bit. She takes them out and says, "Okay. You're a medium."

A girl and four of her friends go out shopping. They spend all day in the mall then get into the girl's car to go home. Suddenly the girl remembers she forgot to buy some condoms. Her boyfriend is coming home after a trip away so she'll need them. She hurries to the nearest pharmacy, grabs a box of condoms, then finds there's a huge line at the checkout. She runs to the front of the line, hands over the condoms and says, "Do you mind if I butt in and buy these? Only I've got four people waiting in my car ... "

What do you call a woman who's allergic to latex?

Mommy.

The World's Shortest Fairy Story: Once upon a time a girl said to a man, "Marry me?" The man said, "No." And the girl went shopping whenever she liked, went out when she wanted, always had a neat house, never had to cook, stayed thin and lived happily ever after.

Other Ulysses Press Books

The Big Ass Book of Jokes
Rudy A. Swale, $14.95

The thousands of jokes in this huge volume range from clean enough to tell at work to too off-color for corporate email. With so many jokes in one book, there is something for everyone.

Blonde Walks into a Bar: The 4,000 Most Hilarious, Gut-Busting Jokes on Everything from Hung-Over Accountants to Horny Zebras
Jonathan Swan, $14.95

Unapologetically funny and irreverent, this book holds nothing back as it delivers laugh after laugh.

The Ginormous Book of Dirty Jokes: Over 1,000 Sick, Filthy and X-Rated Jokes
Rudy A. Swale, $12.95

This masterpeice offers the biggest, baddest, badassest collection of off-color quips.

The Girl's-Only Dirty Joke Book
Karen S. Smith, $10.95

From under-sized penises and unfaithful men to over-sized breasts and less-than-brilliant blondes, this book serves up the filthiest female humor ever put into print.

Man Walks into a Bar: Over 6,000 of the Most Hilarious Jokes, Funniest Insults and Gut-Busting One-Liners
Stephen Arnott & Mike Haskins, $14.95

This book is packed full of quick and easy jokes that are as simple to remember and repeat as they are funny.

The Ultimate Dirty Joke Book
Mike Oxbent & Harry P. Ness, $11.95

This joke collection holds back nothing and guarantees outrageous laughs.

To order these books call 800-377-2542 or 510-601-8301, fax 510-601-8307, e-mail ulysses@ulyssespress.com, or write to Ulysses Press, P.O. Box 3440, Berkeley, CA 94703. All retail orders are shipped free of charge. California residents must include sales tax. Allow two to three weeks for delivery.